1 00

JAPANESE COOKING

Compiled by Judith Ferguson
Tested and Prepared by Jacqueline Bellefontaine
Photographed by Peter Barry
Designed by Philip Clucas
Produced by Ted Smart and
    David Gibbon

CLB 1564
© 1987 Colour Library Books Ltd.,
    Guildford, Surrey, England.
First published in the U.S.A. 1986
    by Exeter Books
Distributed by Bookthrift
Exeter is a trademark of Bookthrift
    Marketing, Inc.
Bookthrift is a registered trademark of
    Bookthrift Marketing, Inc.
New York, New York
Printed and bound in Barcelona, Spain by Cronion, S.A.
ISBN 0-671-08891-2

JAPANESE COOKING

Exeter Books

NEW YORK

CONTENTS

Hors d'Oeuvres 7

Soups 13

Raw Fish 19

Broiling and Pan Frying 22

Steaming and Baking 28

Simmering and One-Pot Cooking 34

Deep Frying 42

Vinegared Foods and Salads 48

Rice, Noodles and Pickles 53

Desserts 60

Index 64

The words simplicity and elegance define Japanese cooking best. With no complicated sauces to distract from the main ingredients, Japanese cooking calls for a few perfect ingredients, exquisitely prepared. Garnishes are kept to a minimum, but they are like miniature sculptures. The Japanese love of pure ingredients stems from the people's love and reverence for nature and all that comes from it. Often, food is garnished with leaves, pine needles or sea plants to remind each person of its origins. Study the artistic arrangement of a Japanese dish and you will see the roots of nouvelle cuisine.

The chapters in this book follow the order of courses at a formal Japanese banquet. Each of the following courses illustrates an important technique in Japanese cooking:

1 Zensai – hors d'oeuvres
2 Sumashi-jiru – clear soups (we have combined this course with miso soups, which normally appear later in the meal)
3 Sashimi – raw fish and garnishes
4 Yakimono – broiled and pan-fried food
5 Mushimono – steamed and baked food
6 Nimono – simmered food
7 Agemono – deep-fried food (Nabemono, one pot dishes such as Sukiyaki, are included in the chapter on simmered food, and sometimes take the place of courses 4-7)

8 Sunomo or Aemono – vinegared food and salads
9 Gohan – rice
10 Miso-shiru – miso soups
11 Tsukemono – pickles
12 Green tea
13 Fresh fruit or desserts

If the number of courses seems daunting, remember that each course is a small serving by Western standards, and that two or three courses can make an excellent meal on their own. Also, don't imagine that you need a vast kitchen filled with specialized equipment – average kitchens in Japan are small, with very basic appliances – everyday kitchen utensils are quite adequate, and sharp knives are an absolute must. Woks are not traditional Japanese cookware, but they adapt well for steaming or frying. Ingredients do not have to be unusual, merely as fresh and good looking as possible, to maintain the Japanese standard. It is, however, useful to have a basic understanding of the following Japanese ingredients:

Adzuki beans – Small dried red beans. Used in rice dishes and sweets.
Agar-agar – Vegetable gelatin sold in blocks or powder. Needs soaking in liquid before use. Use normal gelatin.
Bamboo shoots – First shoots of the bamboo plant. Fresh shoots are best, but the canned variety is more readily

available. Rinse canned shoots before use.

Bonito flakes, dried – Used to make dashi, the basic stock for soups and simmering. Also sprinkled on food to garnish. Sold pre-packaged, the flakes are made from fillets of a mackerel-like fish.

Daikon – A large, white radish, used cooked or raw. Often used grated as a garnish or ingredient in a dipping sauce. Do not substitute pink or red radishes.

Ginger – Knobbly root with a spicy, hot taste. Peel and grate for use. Pickled ginger is often used as a garnish, grated or sliced, for broiled meats. Red or pink in its pickled form.

Glutinous rice – A round-grain variety which cooks to a sticky consistency essential for sushi or vinegared-rice dishes and for picking up with chopsticks. Short-grain rice can be substituted. Rice is so important in Japanese cooking that it is used as a course in itself. For plain boiled rice use long-grain or Patna rice.

Kamaboko – Fish paste sold in a rectangular cake, tinted pink or light green with a white center.

Konbu – A greenish-brown kelp and an important flavoring in dashi. Sold dried, it should be stored tightly covered.

Konnyaku – Gelatinous vegetable paste formed into a cake. It absorbs tastes and colors of foods it is cooked with. Stored in water, it will keep for up to two weeks if the water is changed every day.

Lotus root – Root of the waterlily. Cross-section slice looks like a flower. Available fresh or canned from Japanese groceries.

Mirin – Fermented soy bean paste. Used as a soup base, condiment, sauce ingredient or salad dressing. It comes in a light or white variety, or dark, reddish color. A yellow variety is the most common.

Noodles – Harusame are transparent noodles made from rice. Shirataki noodles are made from devil's tongue root. Both are often called cellophane noodles. Soba are buckwheat noodles. Udon are white noodles made from wheat flour and vary in length and thickness. Somen noodles are the thinnest. Both buckwheat and udon noodles are available dried or fresh in vacuum-sealed packs.

Nori – Laver (seaweed) used to wrap sushi, or shredded to use as a garnish. Sold in thin sheets.

Sesame seeds – Both black and white varieties are used.

Seven-taste (or spice) pepper – A combination of red pepper, sanso pepper, ground orange peel, sesame seed, hemp seed, poppy seed and ground nori seaweed. Usually used to season food at the table.

Shiitake mushroom – Available fresh or dried, the latter being the more common form. Dried mushrooms must be soaked in water for 30 minutes before use, and the stems are removed before cooking.

Shiso leaves – Bright green leaves from a small herb plant. Used as a garnish and available fresh from Japanese groceries. They have a mint-like flavor.

Soy sauce – Japanese type is lighter and sweeter than Chinese. Light variety is saltier than the dark.

Tofu – White cake made from soy bean curd, and custard-like in texture. Usually sold in water-packed cartons, it needs to be thoroughly drained before use. Can be stored in the refrigerator if kept in water that is changed daily.

Trefoil – A herb related to parsley. Use salad cress as a substitute.

Vinegar – Made from rice and pale yellow in color.

Wasabi horseradish – Pale green powdered root with a very hot, pungent taste. Mix with water to a smooth paste and shape into mounds or small leaf shapes. Use as an accompaniment to sashimi or an addition to dipping sauce.

Japanese garnishes are beautiful and, with practice, not difficult to make. The following are the easiest and the ones used in these recipes:

Carrot spurs – Cut a carrot into 3 inch sections and peel. Place in boiling water for about 4 minutes. Carve lengthwise with a sharp knife or dannelle knife. Cut triangular grooves down the length of each carrot. Cut crosswise into slices.

Carrot twists – Cut carrot into 3 inch sections and peel. Slice thinly, lengthwise. Make a 1 inch slit in the center of each slice. Soak the pieces in salt water for at least 10 minutes. Rinse. When pieces are pliable, slip one end of each piece through the slit in the middle and pull back.

Carrot blossoms – Cut carrot in 3 inch sections. Slice five sides to form a pentagon. with a knife or cannelle knife make five lengthwise triangular cuts on all five sides. Trim the top of the carrot so that one end is higher than the other. Slice the flowers thinly, turning as you slice. Go around twice to make double flowers.

Cucumber twigs – Cut 2 inch sections from an unpeeled cucmber. Slice one side lengthwise off this section, about ¼ inch thick. Cut a center section from this piece about 2 inches wide. In this section, make two lengthwise cuts from either end. Do not cut all the way through. Each cut should end ¼ inch from the opposite end. Twist the two outer strips so that they cross over. The same thing can be done with a thick piece of lemon rind.

Zucchini fan or comet – cut the ends off. Slice in half, lengthwise. Make a series of cuts, close together down the length of one half, leaving a spine along the side to hold the slices together. Soak in salt water for at least 10 minutes. Rinse. Spread out on a serving plate. Add a carrot spur.

Radish flowers – Cut stems and tips from radishes. Make two cuts in each of the four sides. Tip should be uppermost. Cut a cross in the top. Soak in ice water until the slice opens.

Radish fans – Choose radishes with leaves. Cut the tip off the radish and cut lengthwise, but not quite through to the leaf end. Soak in salt water and spread out on a plate.

Radish jacks – Slice a radish into thin rounds, Cut a notch in each slice. Slide one slice into the notch of the other.

Lemon and cucumber whirls – Thinly slice lemons and cucumbers. Notch each slice and twist.

Scored mushrooms – Soak dried shiitake mushrooms in hot water for 30 minutes. Cut off the stems and make a cross in the middle of the top of each cap.

HORS D'OEUVRES

Lemon-Ikura

PREPARATION TIME: 5 minutes

SERVES: 4 people

4 rounded tsps salmon roe (large grain)
4 thin slices lemon
2 chives, very finely shredded

Arrange the lemon slices on a serving dish. Mound a spoonful of roe on top of each slice. Garnish each with a few shreds of chive. Serve cold as part of a selection of hors d'oeuvres.

Fresh Vegetables with Sauces

PREPARATION TIME: 30 minutes

COOKING TIME: 2 minutes

SERVES: 4 people

Selection of the following:
Pea pods (2 per person, stems trimmed)
Zucchini (if small, 1 per person, sliced in half. If large, cut 1 into thin strips)
Carrots (as for zucchini)
Green beans (2 per person, stems trimmed)
Shiitake mushrooms, dried (1 per person, cut in quarters if large)
Daikon radish (as for carrots)
Turnips (1 large or 2 small, peeled, quartered and sliced)
Leeks (1 small thin one cut into 1 inch pieces)

SOY AND LEMON SAUCE
6 tbsps soy sauce
4 tbsps fresh lemon juice

SESAME SAUCE
3 tbsps white sesame seeds

2 tbsps mirin
6 tbsps soy sauce
4 tbsps dashi

Fresh Vegetables with Sauces.

Place the vegetables in a steamer or on a rack above boiling water. Cover well and cook 2 minutes. Mix the ingredients for each sauce and divide the mixture among 8 small bowls. Arrange the vegetables attractively on 4 serving plates and serve with the dipping sauces.

Shrimp in Nori Packages

PREPARATION TIME: 20 minutes

COOKING TIME: 2 minutes

SERVES: 4 people

4 jumbo shrimp

This page: Lemon-Ikura. Facing page: Pink, White and Green Rolls (top) and Shrimp in Nori Packages (bottom).

1 square nori
4 chives

BROILING SAUCE
2 tbsps soy sauce
1 tbsp mirin
1 tbsp grated ginger squeezed for juice

GARNISH
Zucchini fan (see introduction)

Shell and de-vein the shrimp, but leave on the tail ends. Pass the sheet of nori over a gas flame on both sides to freshen it. Cut it into 4 strips. Mix all the sauce ingredients together and brush the shrimp. Brush the nori strips and wrap one around each shrimp, but do not completely cover. Place under a pre-heated broiler and cook for 1 minute on each side, brushing with the remaining sauce. Tie each with 1 chive. If desired, prepare double quantity sauce and use some for dipping. Garnish with prepared zucchini fan.

Tofu-Dengaku

PREPARATION TIME: 20 minutes

COOKING TIME: 5-6 minutes

SERVES: 4 people

3oz tofu, well drained, pressed for
    15 minutes and sliced into rectangles
    2 inches long and ½ inch thick
1½ tbsps miso
1½ tbsps mirin
1½ tbsps dashi
½ oz spinach, cooked and puréed or
    defrosted and well drained
1 tbsp white sesame seeds

GARNISH
Radish flower (see introduction)

Prepare the garnish. Place the tofu in a steamer or on a rack above boiling water. Cover and cook for 5-6 minutes. Combine the remaining ingredients, except spinach and sesame seeds, in a small pan and cook slowly until very thick. Add the spinach and mix well. Place tofu on serving dishes and insert small

bamboo skewers lengthwise. Spread the spinach mixture evenly over each piece of tofu and sprinkle with sesame seeds. Garnish with radish flower.

Chicken Livers with Cucumber

PREPARATION TIME: 25 minutes

COOKING TIME: 5-6 minutes

SERVES: 4-6 people

1 tbsp oil
6oz chicken livers, picked over and
    trimmed
2 tsps grated ginger, squeezed for juice
2 tsps mirin
2 tsps soy sauce
½ cucumber, peeled in stripes
1 tbsp white sesame seeds

Heat the oil in a frying pan. Cut the chicken livers into even-sized pieces, but not too small. Put into the hot oil and cook over high heat, turning frequently to brown on the outside. Pour in the soy sauce, mirin and ginger juice and continue to cook 1-2 minutes over medium heat. Livers may be served slightly pink inside. Toss half the livers with sesame seeds to coat. Cut the cucumber half in quarters, lengthwise, and then into pieces the size of the livers. Thread one sesame-seed-coated liver, one piece of cucumber and one plain liver onto small bamboo skewers to serve.

Pink, White and Green Rolls

PREPARATION TIME: 30 minutes, plus chilling time

COOKING TIME: 2 minutes

SERVES: 8 people

3 inch piece of daikon (white) radish,
    peeled
8 large or 16 small spinach leaves
4oz smoked salmon, thinly sliced
Pinch salt

3 tbsps rice vinegar
3 tbsps sugar

Trim the piece of daikon radish into a large cube. Cut the cube into 16 very thin slices. Soak in 2 cups water with 2 tsps salt for about 20 minutes to soften. Wash spinach leaves well and remove thick stalks. Cook 2 minutes in a covered saucepan with a pinch of salt until just wilted. Rinse in cold water and pat dry. Place the salmon slices in 4 rows. Place the spinach leaves, evenly divided, on top of the salmon. Divide the radish slices evenly among the four rows and place on top of the spinach. Roll up and secure with wooden picks. Mix the vinegar and sugar and pour over the rolls. Refrigerate for 2-3 hours, turning once or twice. When ready to serve, remove the picks and slice each roll in half, crosswise. Serve cut side up so that a spiral of pink, white and green shows.

Beef and Scallion Rolls

PREPARATION TIME: 25 minutes

COOKING TIME: 12-15 minutes

SERVES: 4 people

4-6 green onions, trimmed and cut into
    2 inch lengths
4oz sirloin, fat trimmed, sliced very thin
    and cut into 5 x 2 inch pieces
1 tbsp oil
2 tbsps soy sauce
1 tbsp sugar
1 tbsp saké
1 tbsp dashi
1 tbsp mirin

GARNISH
Carrot blossoms (see introduction)
Cucumber twigs (see introduction)

Prepare the garnishes. Divide onions equally into 4-6 groups. Roll 1 slice of beef around 1 group of onions. Tie

**Facing page: Tofu-Dengaku (top)
and Chicken Livers with
Cucumber (bottom).**

rolls with string. Repeat with remaining onions and beef. Heat oil in a large heavy-based frying pan. Add the beef rolls, seam side down, and cook about 1 minute over moderate heat. Turn the rolls several times to brown evenly. Reduce the heat and add all remaining ingredients except the mirin. Cook a further 3 minutes and remove the meat with a slotted spoon. Turn up the heat and cook the pan juices to reduce by half. Add the mirin. Remove the string from the rolls and return them to the pan. Cook the rolls, turning them often, until well

This page: Beef and Scallion Rolls.

glazed. Cut each roll into ½ inch thick rounds. Thread the rounds on skewers and garnish.

JAPANESE COOKING

SOUPS

Summer Chilled Miso Soup

PREPARATION TIME: 25 minutes plus chilling time

COOKING TIME: 25 minutes – 1 hour

SERVES: 4 people

4 cups chicken stock or dashi
3oz miso
½ small cucumber, thinly sliced
1-2 tomatoes, skinned and sliced
½ oz salad cress

Make the stock as for Sumashi Jiru or dashi as for Butaniku no Dango. Chill thoroughly. Cream the miso with about 1 cup of the stock and add to the remaining stock with all the remaining ingredients.

Butaniku no Dango

PREPARATION TIME: 20 minutes

COOKING TIME: 15 minutes

SERVES: 4 people

DASHI
6 cups water
½ oz konbu seaweed
½ oz shaved, dried bonito fillet

8oz ground pork
½ tsp ground ginger
2 tbsps soy sauce
½ oz somen noodles
4 green onions shredded

This page: **Sumashi Jiru (Basic Clear Soup) (top) and Butaniku no Dango (bottom).**

Bring the water to the boil in a
heavy-based pan, add the seaweed
and simmer gently 1-2 minutes.
Remove the seaweed and add the
bonito flakes. Bring back to the boil
and then remove from the heat.
Allow the bonito flakes to sink to the
bottom of the pan and then strain
the stock through cheesecloth, or a
fine-meshed strainer. Combine the
pork and ginger and form into small
balls. Return the stock to the rinsed-
out pan. Add the soy sauce and bring
the stock back to the boil. Add the
pork balls, cover and simmer gently
for 5 minutes. Add the noodles and
continue simmering for 5 minutes,
until the meat balls and noodles are
cooked. Add the green onions and
serve.

**This page: Summer Chilled Miso
Soup. Facing page: Soup with Fish
Dumplings (top) and Shrimp
Noodle Soup (bottom).**

Shrimp Noodle Soup

PREPARATION TIME: 20 minutes

COOKING TIME: 25-35 minutes

SERVES: 4 people

STOCK
8oz fish trimmings (head, bones and skin)
1 small onion, studded with 6 cloves
1 small piece ginger root
5 cups water

SOUP
Strained stock
1oz soba noodles
8oz cooked, peeled shrimp

GARNISH
Parsley sprigs

Place all the stock ingredients into a heavy-based pan. Bring to the boil and simmer gently for 20-25 minutes. Do not over-boil or stock will taste bitter. Remove scum from the surface and strain through cheesecloth, or a fine-meshed strainer. Return the stock to the rinsed-out pan. Add the noodles and simmer for 5-10 minutes until they are cooked. Add the shrimp to the hot soup and pour into individual dishes to serve. Garnish with small sprigs of parsley.

Vegetable Miso Soup

PREPARATION TIME: 30 minutes

COOKING TIME: 25 minutes – 1 hour

SERVES: 4 people

4 cups dashi or chicken stock
2 tbsps oil
4oz daikon radish, cut into matchsticks
2 carrots, peeled and cut into matchsticks
1 small onion, diced
4 whole okra, stems removed and cut into rounds
4 dried mushrooms, soaked 30 minutes, stalks removed
4oz miso

Make stock as for Sumashi Jiru or dashi as for Butaniku no Dango. Heat oil in a heavy-based pan and sauté radish, carrot and onion. When soft, add the okra, mushrooms (with caps scored if desired), and stock or dashi. Bring almost to the boil and mix about 1 cup of the hot stock with the miso. Add this slowly back to the soup. Remove from heat and serve.

Sumashi Jiru (Basic Clear Soup)

PREPARATION TIME: 20 minutes

COOKING TIME: 55 minutes – 1 hour 10 minutes

SERVES: 4 people

STOCK
1 chicken carcass or about 1lb chicken trimmings (bones, giblets, skin etc.)
1 carrot, peeled and roughly chopped
1 small onion, peeled and roughly chopped
2 sticks celery
4 cups water

SOUP
Stock (as above), strained
1 tbsp sherry
2 tbsps soy sauce
4oz diced, cooked chicken
1 medium carrot
4 sprigs watercress

Break the chicken bones into small pieces and add with the remaining stock ingredients to a heavy-based pan. Bring to the boil and then simmer gently for 45 minutes to 1 hour, occasionally skimming off fat if necessary. Strain through cheesecloth, or a fine-meshed strainer. Return to the rinsed out pan. Peel the carrot for the soup and pare off small strips with a cannelle knife, or small paring knife, down the length of the carrot. Cut the carrot into slices to form "flowers". Bring the stock to the boil and add the sherry and soy sauce. Season with salt and pepper, if necessary. Add the carrot flowers and chicken and cook gently for 5-10 minutes until the chicken is hot and the carrot is just tender. Pour into individual bowls and garnish with watercress.

Miso Soup with Shrimp and Fried Tofu

PREPARATION TIME: 25 minutes

COOKING TIME: 25 minutes – 1 hour

SERVES: 4 people

4 cups chicken stock or dashi
2 tbsps oil
4oz tofu, drained and cubed
4 tbsps miso
4oz shrimp
2 green onions, sliced diagonally

GARNISH
4 unshelled shrimp

Make stock as for Sumashi Jiru or dashi as for Butaniku no Dango. Heat the oil in a frying pan and fry the tofu 2 minutes. Remove from the pan and pour over boiling water to remove excess oil. Drain. Heat most of the stock or dashi in a heavy-based pan until just boiling. Remove from the heat. Mix the remaining stock or dashi with miso and add gradually to the pan. Add the tofu and shrimp and garnish with sliced green onion and whole shrimp.

Soup with Fish Dumplings

PREPARATION TIME: 25 minutes

COOKING TIME: 25-35 minutes

SERVES: 4 people

STOCK
12oz-1lb whole whitefish (to give 4oz fillets)
1 small onion, studded with 6 cloves
1 small piece ginger root
5 cups water

¼ tsp ground ginger
2 green onions

Facing page: Miso Soup with Shrimp and Fried Tofu (top) and Vegetable Miso Soup (bottom).

1 egg white
4-5 tbsps (approx) all-purpose flour
2 tbsps oil
4 spears asparagus cut diagonally into
    1 inch pieces
Salt and pepper
Rind and juice of 1 lemon
1 tbsp soy sauce

Fillet and skin the fish, using the
trimmings to make stock as for
Shrimp Noodle Soup. Mince the fish
fillets in a food processor with the
ground ginger, green onions, egg
white, salt and pepper. Gradually
blend in flour until mixture is stiff
enough to shape into small balls. The
mixture will be sticky. Heat the oil in
a heavy-based pan and sauté the
asparagus until just tender. Add the

stock and return to the boil gently.
Carefully add the fish dumplings,
lemon rind and juice and soy sauce,
and simmer for 5-10 minutes until
cooked. Serve immediately.

Clear Tofu Soup

PREPARATION TIME: 20 minutes

COOKING TIME: 55 minutes – 1 hour

SERVES: 4 people

4 cups chicken stock or dashi
3 tbsps soy sauce
4oz tofu, drained and cubed

This page: Clear Tofu Soup. Facing
page: Salmon or Tuna Sashimi.

2 small leeks, washed, trimmed and sliced
2oz bean sprouts

Make up stock as for Sumashi Jiru
(Basic Clear Soup) or dashi as for
Butaniku no Dango. Bring to the boil
in a heavy-based pan and add soy
sauce and leek slices. Simmer until
leeks are tender. Divide between
individual dishes and add the tofu
and bean sprouts to the hot soup.
Serve immediately.

RAW FISH

Tuna Sashimi

PREPARATION TIME: 50 minutes

SERVES: 4 people

8oz tuna fillet
½ cup light soy sauce

GARNISH
Carrot twists (see introduction)
Cellophane noodles

Prepare the carrot twists. Skin the fillets and treat as in Salmon Sashimi. Slice the tuna across the grain. Place in shallow serving bowls. Cover cellophane noodles with hot water and soak for 5 minutes. Drain and leave to cool. Arrange carrot twists and a portion of cellophane noodles next to the tuna on each plate.

Salmon or Tuna Sashimi

PREPARATION TIME: 50 minutes

SERVES: 4 people

8oz raw salmon or tuna fillet
½ daikon radish, finely grated

SAUCE
6 tbsps soy sauce
3 tbsps lemon juice

GARNISH
4 zucchini fans (see introduction)
4 carrot spurs (see introduction)

Skin the fish fillet, place in a colander and pour over boiling water. This will not cook the fish. Place immediately into ice-cold water. Pat the fish dry and slice across the grain into ⅜ inch-thick strips. Arrange daikon radish in mounds in 4 serving bowls. Place the slices of fish against the daikon radish mounds. Mix the soy sauce and lemon juice and divide into 4 small bowls. Garnish with prepared zucchini fans and carrot spurs arranged to look like a comet.

Scallop Sashimi

PREPARATION TIME: 50 minutes

SERVES: 4 people

4 large or 8 small, fresh scallops with roe, if possible
4 shiso leaves
4 lemon twigs (see introduction)
2 tbsps wasabi horseradish powder mixed with water to a thick paste

SAUCE
6 tbsps light soy sauce
2 tbsps lemon juice

Wash the scallops in cold, salted water. Pat dry and slice into very thin rounds, leaving the roe in one piece. Overlap slices of scallops in serving dish or place roe on one side. Decorate with shiso leaves and lemon twigs. Mix the soy sauce and

lemon juice together and serve one bowl of the sauce with each serving of sashimi.

Squid Sashimi

PREPARATION TIME: 50 minutes

SERVES: 4 people

1 squid (prepared squid are available from fishmongers and Japanese markets)
1 carrot, finely grated

SAUCE
½ cup soy sauce
Pinch wasabi powder

GARNISH
Fennel or dill fronds
4 radish fans (see introduction)

Prepare the radish fans. Wash the squid in cold, salted water and pat dry. Lightly score one side of the squid and then cut into ⅜ inch-thick strips, crosswise. Place a mound of

carrot on each serving dish. Place the squid against the mound of carrot. Mix the soy sauce and the wasabi and pour into 4 small bowls. Garnish with fennel or dill and prepared radish fans.

This page: Tuna Sashimi. Facing page: Scallop Sashimi (top) and Squid Sashimi (bottom).

JAPANESE COOKING

BROILING AND PAN-FRYING

Beef and Leek Skewers

PREPARATION TIME: 25 minutes

COOKING TIME: 8-10 minutes

SERVES: 4 people

1lb butt steak, cut in 1½ inch cubes
4 leeks, cut in 1½ inch pieces, white and
    pale green part only
3 tbsps oil
4 tbsps sugar
2 tbsps mirin
1 tbsp grated ginger
½ cup soy sauce
Pinch black pepper

GARNISH
Lemon slices

Thread the leeks and beef alternately
onto bamboo skewers. This should
fill 2-3 skewers per person. Pour oil
into a large frying pan. When hot,
add 2 skewers at a time and brown all
sides well, about 1-2 minutes. Drain
off any excess oil and mix the
remaining ingredients. Pour over the
meat and cook a further 2-3 minutes.
Remove the meat and simmer until
the sauce is thick and syrupy, about
5 minutes. Pour over the meat and
garnish with lemon slices.

Chicken Yakitori

PREPARATION TIME: 30 minutes

COOKING TIME: 5-6 minutes

SERVES: 4 people

4 tbsps mirin
4 tbsps sake
½ cup soy sauce

Pinch cayenne pepper
1 clove garlic
1 small piece ginger
1 tsp sugar

**This page: Chicken Yakitori. Facing
page: Pork Kebabs with Vegetables
(top) and Beef and Leek Skewers
(bottom).**

1 chicken, skinned, boned and cut in
    1 inch pieces
2 large green peppers, cored, seeded and
    cut in 1 inch pieces
2-4 leeks, depending on size (substitute
    green onions when leeks are out of
    season)

GARNISH
Radish jacks (see introduction)

Combine the first 7 ingredients in a small pan and bring to the boil. Remove from the heat and set aside to cool. Pour over the chicken and marinate for 30 minutes. Wash the leeks well and cut off the dark green tops. Cut the white and pale green parts into 1 inch pieces. If the leeks are very thick, cut in half. Thread 2 pieces of chicken onto bamboo or metal skewers, followed by a piece of pepper and leek, until all the ingredients are used. This will make 2-3 skewers per person. Reserve the marinade. Pre-heat a broiler and cook the chicken skewers 5-6 minutes per side, basting frequently with the marinade. May be cooked on a charcoal grill as well. Garnish with radish jacks.

Pork Kebabs with Vegetables

PREPARATION TIME: 30 minutes

COOKING TIME: 5-6 minutes

SERVES: 4 people

1 small eggplant
2 green peppers
1 onion, cut in 1 inch pieces
12oz pork tenderloin

SAUCE
2 tbsps oil
2 tbsps soy sauce
3 tbsps Worcestershire sauce
3 tbsps ketchup
1 tbsp grated ginger, squeezed for juice
1 clove garlic, finely minced

GARNISH
Lemon and cucumber twists (see
    introduction)

Slice the eggplant in half and score lightly. Sprinkle with salt and leave to stand 30 minutes. Cut the peppers in half and remove seeds. Cut into 1 inch pieces. Cut the pork into 1 inch pieces. Squeeze the juices from the eggplant and rinse well. Pat dry and cut into pieces the size of the pork. Thread the ingredients onto bamboo or metal skewers, beginning with pork and alternating between pork and vegetables, ending with pork. This should make 2-3 kebabs per person. Mix the sauce ingredients thoroughly. Brush the kebabs and place under a pre-heated broiler. Cook 5-6 minutes, turning every 2 minutes, until the pork is cooked. Brush frequently with the sauce. Serve remaining sauce in separate bowls. Garnish with lemon and cucumber twists.

Beef Teriyaki

PREPARATION TIME: 30 minutes

COOKING TIME: 12-14 minutes

SERVES: 4 people

Light cooking oil, such as soya or peanut
    oil
1 large onion, sliced
4 very small zucchini, ends trimmed
8 small or 4 large mushrooms, halved and
    scored
4 butt steaks about 4oz in weight

SAUCE
4 tbsps dark soy sauce
4 tbsps sake
3 tbsps mirin
1 clove garlic, finely chopped
1 small piece ginger, finely chopped

Pour about 2 tbsps oil into a large frying pan. When hot, place in the onion slices in one layer. Fry until golden brown on both sides, about 1-2 minutes. Remove and keep warm. Cut the zucchini into thin rounds. Add 2 tbsps more oil to the pan and cook the zucchini quickly over high heat. Set aside and add the mushrooms to the pan. Cook 1 minute and set aside. Keep all the

vegetables warm while cooking the steaks. Add more oil to the pan and keep the heat high. Cook 1 steak at a time until both sides are brown, about 1 minute per side. Put all the steaks into the pan, pour over the sauce and cover. Cook over moderate heat 1-2 minutes. Divide all the vegetables evenly among 4 plates. Place steaks on the plates and cut in half, lengthwise, then into about 8 short strips. Pour the sauce over the steaks to serve.

Tuna Teriyaki

PREPARATION TIME: 20 minutes

COOKING TIME: 17 minutes

SERVES: 4 people

4 tuna fish steaks
2 tbsps oil
4 tbsps soy sauce
1 tbsp mirin
1 tbsp sugar
1 tbsp miso

GARNISH
Radish flowers and leaves (see
    introduction)

Heat the oil in a large frying pan. Add the tuna and cook until slightly browned, about 2 minutes. Drain away excess oil and add the soy sauce, mirin and sugar. Cook over very low heat to cook the fish, about 5 minutes. Remove the fish from the pan and keep warm. Cook liquid over high heat to reduce by half. Stir in the miso. Skin tuna steaks and separate carefully in half. Discard bones and skin. Pour sauce over the fish and garnish with radish flowers and leaves.

Facing page: Beef Teriyaki (top) and Tuna Teriyaki (bottom).

Broiled Green Peppers

PREPARATION TIME: 15 minutes

COOKING TIME: 4-5 minutes

SERVES: 4 people

4 medium-sized green peppers
2 tbsps oil
Sesame seeds
Pickled ginger

Quarter the peppers and remove the seeds and cores. Heat a broiler and brush the peppers on all sides with oil. Cook for 4-5 minutes, turning the peppers every minute. During the last minute of cooking, turn the peppers skin side up and sprinkle over the sesame seeds. Allow the seeds to brown slightly and then remove the peppers to a serving dish. Serve with grated pickled ginger, if desired.

Flying Fish

PREPARATION TIME: 40 minutes

COOKING TIME: 4-10 minutes

SERVES: 4 people

4 fresh small sea bream, trout or red
*   mullet*
Salt
Soy sauce

GARNISH
4 shiso leaves
4 lemon twigs

Scale the fish and gut them through the gills (a fishmonger will prepare the fish in this way). Rinse the fish very well and pat dry. Place the fish with the heads all pointing to the right and the stomach in front of you. Starting just behind the eye area, thread one or two metal skewers 3 times through 1 side of the fish. Do not allow the skewers to penetrate both sides of the fish. Bend the fish slightly every time the skewers are threaded through. Rub salt into the fins to make them stand up. Coat the tail with salt as well. Make sure the salt coating is quite heavy. Pre-heat a broiler and place the fish on a rack, the side not penetrated by skewers

uppermost. Broil 2-5 minutes per side. Twist the skewers occasionally to make them easier to remove. Place the fish on individual serving plates with the side broiled first uppermost. Remove the skewers and garnish with the shiso leaves and lemon twigs. Serve the soy sauce in individual bowls for dipping.

Egg Roll

PREPARATION TIME: 20 minutes

COOKING TIME: 1-2 minutes

SERVES: 3 people

4 eggs, beaten
⅓ cup dashi
Pinch salt
¼ tsp light soy sauce
2 green onions, roughly chopped
1 shiitake mushroom, roughly chopped
1 sheet nori, finely shredded

GARNISH
½ daikon radish, finely grated

This is best made in a special oblong Japanese omelet pan. A large frying pan may be substituted. Mix the eggs with the dashi, salt and soy sauce. Brush the pan with a light film of oil. Heat until slightly smoking. Pour in enough of the egg to coat the bottom of the pan. Cook for a few seconds, until the egg is just set. Sprinkle over the onions and mushroom. Roll up the omelet and push to one side of the pan. Brush the pan again with oil and pour in more of the egg. Cook again until just set. Roll up the first omelet inside the second and repeat until all the egg is used. Lift out of the pan and cut into nine rolls. Pass the nori over a gas flame on both sides to freshen. Shred finely. Arrange nori strips on plates and place 3 rolls on top. Garnish with a little grated daikon radish.

This page: Flying Fish. Facing page: Egg Roll (top) and Broiled Green Peppers (bottom).

JAPANESE COOKING

STEAMING AND BAKING

Shrimp Egg Custard

PREPARATION TIME: 20 minutes

COOKING TIME: 20-25 minutes

SERVES: 4 people

STOCK
2 cups dashi
1 tsp soy sauce
1 tsp mirin
Pinch salt

4 dried shiitake mushrooms; soaked
* 30 minutes, drained and scored*
4 jumbo shrimp
4 pea pods, blanched and cut in half
1oz bean sprouts
5 eggs, beaten

GARNISH
1 piece pickled ginger, grated

Bring stock ingredients to the boil.
Take off the heat and leave to cool.
Strain the stock and when cool mix
with the beaten eggs. Divide the
mixture evenly among 4 heat-
resistant cups or small bowls. Add
the bean sprouts and position the
shrimp so the tail shows. Add the
pea pods and float a mushroom on
top of the custard. Pour water into a
steamer or a large, deep saucepan and
bring to the boil. Place the cups on a
steamer or a rack above the boiling
water. Cover the pan or steamer and
cook over high heat for about 2
minutes. Reduce the heat and steam
until just set, about 15 minutes. A
toothpick inserted into the middle of

**This page: Shrimp Egg Custard.
Facing page: Steamed Abalone
(top) and Baked Stuffed Trout
(bottom).**

the custard should come out clean when the custard is cooked. Garnish with the pickled ginger.

Baked Stuffed Trout

PREPARATION TIME: 20 minutes

COOKING TIME: 16-19 minutes

OVEN TEMPERATURE:
400°F (200°C)

SERVES: 4 people

4 small trout, cleaned and boned

STUFFING
4 tbsps red miso
2 green onions, chopped
2 tbsps sugar
1 tbsp mirin
1 tbsp dashi
1 tbsp grated ginger

GARNISH
Lime slices

Make sure the heads and tails of the fish are left on. Cut 4 pieces of foil large enough to enclose each fish. Brush lightly with oil. Combine stuffing ingredients in a saucepan. Cook over moderate heat 4 minutes to thicken. Place each fish on a piece of foil and spread the stuffing in the cavity. Fold the foil over the fish tightly and twist the ends. Bake 12-14 minutes. Partially open the foil to serve. Garnish with a slice of lime.

Beef Roasted with Vegetables

PREPARATION TIME: 25 minutes

COOKING TIME: 15 minutes

OVEN TEMPERATURE:
400°F (200°C)

SERVES: 4 people

1lb sirloin or rib roast, sliced in very thin strips

8 shiitake mushrooms, quartered lengthwise
1 green pepper, cored, seeded and cut in 8 pieces, lengthwise
1 carrot, quartered
4 tbsps mirin
4 tbsps soy sauce
Seven spices pepper

DIPPING SAUCE
4 tbsps lemon juice
4 tbsps orange juice
½ cup soy sauce
½ cup dashi

GARNISH
1 small piece daikon radish
1 small red chili pepper
4 shiso leaves
4 orange slices

Cut 4 pieces of foil about 10 inches square. Brush with oil. Place an equal portion of beef, bamboo shoots, peppers, mushroom and carrot on the foil. Mix mirin, soy sauce and seven spice pepper together and pour over each portion. Wrap well and cook 15 minutes. Combine sauce ingredients and pour into 4 small bowls. Remove core from the radish with a vegetable peeler. Insert chili pepper and grate together, finely. Arrange a leaf on each serving plate. Add grated daikon radish and chili pepper and an orange slice. Open the foil packets and place one on each dish. Serve each person with a sauce bowl for dipping.

Steamed Abalone

PREPARATION TIME: 30 minutes

COOKING TIME: 20 minutes

SERVES: 4 people

4 fresh abalone in the shell, if possible
Salt
4 tbsps sake

MISO SAUCE
⅓ cup red miso
4 tbsps dashi
2 tbsps sugar
2 tbsps mirin

GARNISH
4 large pieces konbu seaweed
2oz pickled ginger, sliced

Use a strong spatula to remove the abalone if in the shell. Scrub the shells well and reserve. Sprinkle the abalone liberally with salt and scrub to remove black portion. Peel off green edges with a knife. Lightly score the surface of the abalone and line the shells or serving dishes with the seaweed. Replace the abalone in the shell on top of the seaweed and put into a steamer or on a rack above boiling water. Spoon the sake over each abalone, cover and steam for 20 minutes on moderate heat. Brush with miso sauce after about 12 minutes steaming. Remove the abalone, cut in half horizontally and then into ½ inch strips. Replace in the shells. Garnish with cucumber and ginger. Use any remaining miso sauce as a dipping sauce.

Steamed Chicken

PREPARATION TIME: 25 minutes

COOKING TIME: 15 minutes

SERVES: 4 people

1lb chicken breasts, boned
2 tsps salt
2 tbsps sake
1 tbsp light soy sauce
1 tbsp dark soy sauce

4 leaves of Chinese cabbage
1 piece daikon radish
1 small red pepper

Prick the skin of the chicken and salt lightly. Mix the sake and soy sauce and pour over the chicken. Rub in well. Place chicken in a steamer or in a dish on a rack over boiling water. Cover and cook 15 minutes on moderate heat. Cut into ½ inch strips. Meanwhile, insert a vegetable peeler lengthwise into the daikon radish and remove a core. Push in the

Facing page: Beef Roasted with Vegetables.

pepper. Grate the two together, finely. Place the Chinese cabbage on a plate and arrange the chicken. Garnish with small mounds of grated daikon radish. Reduce the cooking liquid from the chicken by boiling rapidly in a small saucepan. Use as a sauce.

Steamed Fish Rolls

PREPARATION TIME: 25 minutes

COOKING TIME: 10-15 minutes

SERVES: 4 people

2 large sole or flounder to give 4 whole
    fillets
4 green onions, blanched 2 minutes
6oz shrimp
2 tsps cornstarch
1 tsp sake
2 eggs, beaten
Salt

GLAZE
1 tbsp white miso
1 tbsp mirin

GARNISH
1 small piece pickled daikon radish,
    fanned
4 whole shrimp

Skin the fish fillets and lay them skin side up on a flat surface. Chop the shrimp finely and mix with cornstarch and sake. Divide the shrimp filling between the 2 fillets and spoon into a mound across the middle of the fillet. Trim off the white part of the onions and use only the green. Place the onions next to the shrimp filling. Cook the eggs with a pinch of salt until softly scrambled. Place in a mound next to the onions. Roll up the fish fillets, folding the thicker end over the filling first. Secure with wooden picks. Place in the top part of a steamer. Boil water in the bottom part. Alternatively, use a large pan and place the fish on a rack over boiling water. Steam for 10-15 minutes, until the fish is cooked. Five minutes before the end of cooking, brush with combined glaze ingredients. Cut in slices and serve garnished with pickled daikon

radish cut in a fan shape and whole shrimp.

Hakata-Mushi (Steamed Ground Pork)

PREPARATION TIME: 30 minutes

COOKING TIME: 50 minutes

SERVES: 4 people

1lb Chinese cabbage, parboiled 2 minutes
3 eggs, beaten
1lb ground pork
2 tbsps all-purpose flour
1 tbsp soy sauce
Pinch salt

SAUCE
2 cups dashi
3 tbsps soy sauce
½ clove garlic, finely minced
1 tbsp cornstarch

Line the bottom of a greased 1lb loaf pan with ⅓ of the cabbage leaves. Mix ⅓ of the beaten egg with the meat, flour, soy sauce and salt. Pour half of the remaining egg into the pan over the cabbage leaves. Press half of the meat mixture on top of the egg. Cover with another ⅓ of the cabbage leaves and add another layer of meat. Pour remaining egg over the meat and cover with remaining cabbage leaves. Press the mixture down and cover the pan with foil. Bring water to the boil in a steamer or large, deep pan with a tight-fitting lid. Place the pan in the steamer or on a rack above the water and cook 50 minutes, covered. Mix the cornstarch with 2 tbsps of dashi. Bring the remaining dashi to the boil and add the soy sauce and garlic. Gradually stir in the cornstarch and cook, stirring constantly, until the mixture thickens. Cover the surface of the

Facing page: Steamed Chicken (top) and Hakata-Mushi (Steamed Ground Pork) (bottom). This page: Steamed Fish Rolls.

sauce with wax paper to prevent a skin forming. Allow the sauce to cool. Cool the hakata-mushi to room temperature and cut into squares or slices. Serve with the cooled sauce for dipping.

SIMMERING AND ONE-POT COOKING

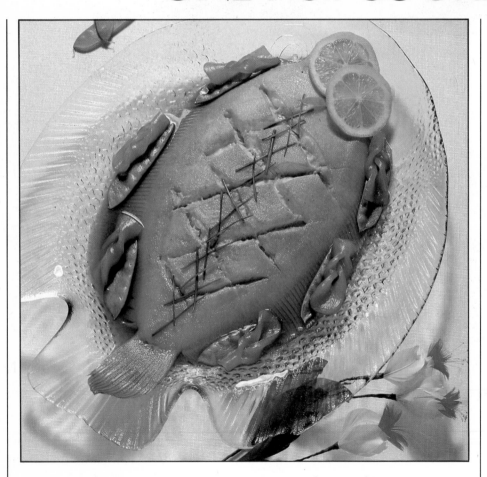

dashi, mirin and soy sauce. Gut the fish or buy already prepared. Leave on the heads and tails. Score the white side of the fish with a sharp knife. Put the fish cut sides down into a large, shallow pan. Pour over the stock and cook gently on top of the heat for 15-20 minutes. Remove the fish to serving dishes and turn cut side up. Keep warm. Cut the konnyaku cake into rectangles about ¼ inch thick. Cut a slit in the middle and pull the end of the konnyaku through the slit, twisting as you pull. Place in the fish cooking liquid and cook 5 minutes on gentle heat. Arrange the blanched pea pods and konnyaku against the fish and spoon some of the cooking liquid over each.

Simmered Flounder

PREPARATION TIME: 35 minutes

COOKING TIME: 27 minutes

SERVES: 4 people

½ cup sake
1½ cups dashi
½ cup mirin
½ cup soy sauce
4 small flounder or sole

4oz pea pods, steamed 2 minutes
1 cake konnyaku

GARNISH
Lemon Slices
Shredded chives

Pour sake into a small saucepan and warm gently. Ignite the fumes and allow to burn until the flames die off naturally. Keep a pan lid handy in case the flames shoot up. Add the

Simmered Vegetables

PREPARATION TIME: 30 minutes

COOKING TIME: 7 minutes

SERVES: 4 people

2lbs of a selection of the following:
Shiitake mushrooms, soaked 30 minutes,
    stalks removed
Turnips, peeled and pared into thick
    barrel shapes
Carrots, peeled

**This page: Simmered Flounder.
Facing page: Simmered Vegetables
(top) and Simmered Coltsfoot and
Carrots (bottom).**

Konnyaku cake, cut in ¼ inch slices
Zucchini cut in ¼ inch diagonal slices
Pea pods, strings removed if necessary,
* ends trimmed on the diagonal*
Green onions, cut in 1 inch diagonal
* pieces*

BROTH
1½ cups dashi
2 tsps sake
4 tbsps soy sauce
3 tbsps mirin

Score the mushroom caps if desired. Use a sharp, small knife to cut the turnips into thick hexagonal shapes. Take strips off the carrots, lengthwise, with a cannelle knife or paring knife. Cut crosswise into "flower" shapes. Cut a lengthwise slit in the konnyaku cake slices. Pull one end through the slit, twisting as you pull. Bring the dashi and sake to the boil in a saucepan and add the turnip and konnyaku. Blanch 1 minute. Remove the vegetables and set aside. Put in the pea pods and zucchini. Blanch 30 seconds. Return the turnips and konnyaku to the pan and add the mushrooms and carrots. Add the sugar, soy sauce and bring to the boil. Allow to simmer 5 minutes. Add the green onions during the last minute of cooking. Remove all the vegetables with a draining spoon and arrange in serving dishes. Allow the sauce to boil rapidly to reduce it. Add the mirin and cook 30 seconds. Allow to cool slightly and pour over the vegetables.

Chicken One Pot

PREPARATION TIME: 35 minutes
COOKING TIME: 30 minutes
SERVES: 6 people

2 tbsps oil
1lb boned chicken, thinly sliced
1 cup chicken stock
4 tbsp soy sauce
2 tbsps sugar
1 carrot, sliced diagonally
1 medium green pepper, cut in thin strips
8oz fresh spinach leaves, well washed
8 shiitake mushrooms, soaked 30 minutes

1 piece tofu, sliced
1 small bunch coriander leaves
8oz buckwheat noodles, cooked

SAUCE AND GARNISH
6 tbsps soy sauce
6 tbsps lemon juice
1 piece daikon radish, peeled and stuck
* with 1 small red chili pepper*

Heat oil in an electric frying pan or chafing dish at the table. Start frying the chicken a few slices at a time. Mix stock, soy sauce and sugar. When chicken pieces are cooked, push to the side of the pan and add some of each vegetable and a small portion of noodles. Moisten all with stock mixture. Make a hole in the center of the daikon radish with a vegetable peeler and push in the chili pepper. Grate the two together finely and serve in small mounds next to mounds of onion. Serve the soy sauce and lemon juice in individual bowls. As the ingredients are cooked, each person takes food from the pan. A bit of the radish and onion may be mixed into the dipping sauce. Dip food into the sauce and continue to cook ingredients as the meal goes on.

Simmered Chicken with Okra

PREPARATION TIME: 20 minutes
COOKING TIME: 12 minutes
SERVES: 4 people

1½ cups dashi or chicken stock
3 tbsps mirin
5 tbsps soy sauce
2 chicken breasts, boned and cut in slivers
½ cup dashi or chicken stock
6 okra pods, stems trimmed and cut in
* rounds*
1 piece tofu, cut in slices
Bamboo shoots cut in thin matchsticks

GARNISH
Carrot flowers (see introduction)

Prepare the garnish. Mix the first 3 ingredients and bring to the boil in a shallow pan. Add the chicken and cook 10 minutes on moderate heat. Take off the heat and set aside. Add remaining dashi to a small saucepan with the okra, tofu and bamboo shoots. Cook 2 minutes. Arrange the chicken and vegetables in shallow serving bowls. Pour over a small amount of chicken cooking liquid. Garnish with carrot flowers.

Simmered Coltsfoot and Carrots

PREPARATION TIME: 25 minutes
COOKING TIME: 14 minutes
SERVES: 4 people

2 coltsfoot stems (4 sticks celery may be
* substituted)*
2 cups dashi
1 tbsp sugar
2 tbsps mirin
2 tbsps soy sauce
1 small carrot, cut in thin ribbons
Bonito flakes

Cook the coltsfoot stems or celery sticks whole in 4 cups salted water. Cook 4 minutes. Rinse under cold water. Peel the stems from the bottom of the coltsfoot and drain. Cut coltsfoot or celery into 2 inch sticks. Combine dashi, sugar, mirin and soy sauce in a saucepan and bring to the boil. Add the coltsfoot and simmer 10 minutes. Simmer only 5 minutes for celery. Add the carrot ribbons 2 minutes before the end of cooking. Remove the vegetables and arrange in dishes. Allow the vegetables and cooking liquid to cool. Pour some of the liquid over each serving of vegetables and serve cold, garnished with bonito flakes.

Facing page: Simmered Chicken with Okra (top) and Chicken One Pot (bottom).

1½ cups dashi
1 tbsp mirin
1 small piece ginger, peeled and left whole

Cut strips from the carrot lengthwise with a cannelle knife or paring knife. Cut the carrot crosswise into ¼ inch "flower" slices. Trim the ends of the beans on the diagonal. Slice the daikon pieces into thin rectangles. Cut the kamaboku paste into slices and cut a lengthwise slit in the middle of each. Pull one end of the paste through the slit, twisting gently. Place the paste and all the vegetables, except the mushrooms, in a shallow pan and cover with water. Add a pinch of salt and cover the pan tightly. Cook about 2 minutes on high heat, until the carrots are almost tender. Add the bamboo shoots halfway through cooking time. Meanwhile, bring the dashi, mirin and ginger to the boil in a shallow pan. Leave the shells on the very ends of the tails of the shrimp. Place them in the hot dashi and cook 2 minutes or until just pink. Do not allow them to boil. Arrange all the ingredients attractively in 4 shallow bowls. Spoon over some of the dashi mixture and serve immediately.

Sukiyaki

PREPARATION TIME: 40 minutes

COOKING TIME: 30 minutes

SERVES: 6 people

6 eggs, beaten
3 tbsps oil
1½ lbs sirloin, sliced paper thin
1 bunch green onions, cut in ½ inch diagonal pieces
8 shiitake mushrooms, soaked 30 minutes and scored
5oz shirataki noodles, soaked 5 minutes and cut in 5 inch lengths
5oz udon noodles, cooked
8oz Chinese cabbage
8oz fresh spinach, leaves washed and stems removed
2 bamboo shoots, cut in triangular pieces
15oz cake konnyaku, sliced
15oz cake tofu, sliced
Salad cress or watercress

Simmered Shrimp with Vegetables

PREPARATION TIME: 30 minutes

COOKING TIME: 2 minutes

SERVES: 4 people

8oz shrimp or 1lb jumbo shrimp
2 medium carrots, peeled
16 green beans

This page: Sukiyaki. Facing page: Cod and Cabbage One Pot (top) and Simmered Shrimp with Vegetables (bottom).

1 small piece daikon radish, cut into matchsticks
1 piece kamaboku fish paste or konnyaku
2oz bamboo shoots, cut into matchsticks

BROTH
1 cup dashi
½ cup soy sauce
3 tbsps mirin
1 tbsp sugar

Break one egg into each of 6 bowls and beat lightly. Arrange all the ingredients on a large tray. Heat oil in an electric frying pan or chafing dish at the table. Brown the meat a few pieces at a time. Add onions. Move meat to one side of the dish and add equal portions of the other ingredients. Mix broth ingredients together and add some to the pan. Each person takes some of the cooked food and dips it into the egg, which quickly glazes the hot food. Keep adding ingredients and simmering liquid as the meal progresses.

Eternity Patties

PREPARATION TIME: 20 minutes

COOKING TIME: 13-15 minutes

SERVES: 4-5 people

12oz ground chicken
½ egg, beaten
2 tbsps all-purpose flour
½ tsp ground ginger
½ cup all-purpose flour
2½ cups dashi
3 tbsps soy sauce
2 tbsps sugar
1 tbsp sake

GARNISH
Radish flowers and leaves

Combine the chicken, egg, 2 tbsps flour, ginger and salt in a large bowl and mix well. Divide the mixture into 10 (mixture will be soft). Lightly flour hands and form mixture into patties. Coat the patties with the remaining flour mixed with a pinch of salt. Score a lattice on the top of each patty using the blunt side of a knife. Combine remaining ingredients in a large frying pan and bring to the boil. Add the patties to the pan, scored side up, and swirl liquid over the tops. Reduce heat and simmer 3-4 minutes. Gently turn the patties over

and cook 5-6 minutes. Turn again and increase the heat to bring the liquid up to a rapid boil. Quickly swirl the liquid over the patties for about 2 minutes. Transfer the patties to a serving dish and spoon over some of the cooking liquid. Garnish with radish flowers and leaves.

Cod and Cabbage One Pot

PREPARATION TIME: 40 minutes

COOKING TIME: 30 minutes

SERVES: 4 people

10 dried shiitake mushrooms, soaked 30 minutes
1lb cod fillet, skinned and cut in 1 inch pieces
3 small leeks, washed and cut in 2½ inch lengths
8oz Chinese cabbage
8oz tofu, drained
1½ oz cellophane noodles, soaked 5 minutes
5 cups dashi

SAUCE
2 tbsps rice vinegar
2 tbsps soy sauce
4 tbsps mirin
2 tbsps lemon juice
4 tbsps sake
1 small piece konbu seaweed

GARNISH
2 green onions, finely chopped
3oz piece daikon radish, stuck with 1 red pepper, finely grated

Drain mushrooms and cut off stalks. Trim down spines of the cabbage leaves and cut the leaves into 3 irregular-shaped pieces. Cut the tofu into 10 pieces. Drain the noodles and arrange all the ingredients on a large tray. Bring the stock to the boil. Mix the sauce ingredients and pour into 4 small bowls. Arrange a mound of onion and one of grated daikon radish on each of 4 separate plates or trays. Put the pot of stock on an electric ring on the table. Add the fish, then the mushrooms and then

the cabbage leaves. Add the leeks, noodles and tofu. Each person mixes small amounts of onion and radish into the sauce and takes food from the main pot to dip into the sauce. A fondue pot may also be used for cooking.

Simmered Pork and Vegetable Casserole

PREPARATION TIME: 25 minutes

COOKING TIME: 1 hour

SERVES: 4 people

2 tbsps oil
1lb pork spare ribs, cut in 1 inch pieces
1oz piece ginger, sliced thinly
3 tbsps sake
4 tbsps soy sauce
2 tbsps sugar
2oz green beans, cut in 2 inch lengths
2 sticks celery, cut in 2 inch lengths
2oz bamboo shoots, cut into strips

Heat the oil in a large sauté pan. Cook the sliced ginger briefly and remove. Add the pork to the pan, turn up the heat and brown on all sides. Pour in water to just barely cover. Return the ginger to the pan. Add the sake, cover and cook for 1 hour. Check the level of liquid and add more water if the meat begins to dry out. When the pork is tender, add the soy sauce, and sugar and cook, uncovered, to reduce the sauce to syrupy consistency. Meanwhile, put beans and celery into a small pan and barely cover with water. Add a pinch of salt and bring to the boil. Cook 2-3 minutes until tender-crisp. Add the bamboo shoots after about 2 minutes. Place the pork in individual serving dishes and scatter over the vegetables. Pour over any remaining sauce.

Facing page: Simmered Pork and Vegetable Casserole (top) and Eternity Patties (bottom).

DEEP-FRYING

Lemony Marinated Herring

PREPARATION TIME: 15 minutes

COOKING TIME: 10-20 minutes

SERVES: 4 people

4 herrings, cleaned and heads removed
3 tbsps rice vinegar
2 tbsps soy sauce
2 tbsps sake
1 tbsp lemon juice
Cornstarch to dredge
Oil for frying

Score the fish diagonally 3 or 4 times on one side. Mix the vinegar, soy sauce, sake and lemon juice together and sprinkle over the fish. Leave in a cool place to marinate for 15 minutes. Heat oil to 350°F (180°C) in a deep-fat fryer or wok. Dredge the fish with cornstarch and fry in the hot oil, 2 fish at a time. Cook for 5-10 minutes. Drain on paper towels. Garnish with lemon and cucumber twigs, if desired.

Deep-Fried Pork

PREPARATION TIME: 15 minutes

COOKING TIME: 5 minutes per batch

SERVES: 4 people

4 slices pork tenderloin, about ½ inch
    thick
Flour with salt and pepper
2 egg whites, lightly beaten
1 cup fresh breadcrumbs
Oil for frying
½ head Chinese cabbage
1 lime, sliced

Clip the edges of the pork slices to prevent curling and dip in the seasoned flour. Shake off excess flour and dip the pork into the egg white and then sprinkle with breadcrumbs.

This page: Taksuta-Age (Deep-Fried Chicken) (top) and Deep-Fried Pork (bottom). Facing page: Snowy Fried Shrimp (top) and Lemon Marinated Herring (bottom).

Heat the oil to 350°F (180°C) in a deep-fat fryer or wok. Fry 1 or 2 slices at a time for about 5 minutes. Remove the pork and drain on paper towels. Slice each piece diagonally into ½ inch thick strips. Serve assembled on a bed of shredded Chinese cabbage and garnish with lime slices.

Snowy Fried Shrimp

PREPARATION TIME: 20 minutes

COOKING TIME: 2 minutes per batch

SERVES: 4 people

1½ lbs cooked jumbo shrimp, peeled
2oz harusame or saifan (soy flour noodles)
½ cup flour with salt and pepper
2 egg whites
Oil for frying

De-vein the shrimp and score diagonally on the underside. Cut the noodles into ¼-½ inch pieces. Beat the egg whites until foamy. Dip the shrimp into the seasoned flour and shake off surplus. Dip into egg white and then sprinkle on the noodles until each shrimp is completely covered. Heat oil in a deep-fat fryer or wok to 325°F (160°C). Add the shrimp to the hot oil and fry a few at a time until the noodles look opaque, about 2 minutes. Drain well before serving. They should not be allowed to brown.

Vegetable Tempura

PREPARATION TIME: 30 minutes

COOKING TIME: 2 minutes per batch

SERVES: 4 people

Selection of the following ingredients prepared as directed:
Celery, cut into sticks
Artichoke hearts, halved
Lotus root, sliced in rounds about ¼ inch thick
Mushrooms, whole fresh or dried, soaked 30 minutes, with stems removed
Green peppers, cut in ¼ inch thick rings or strips
Onions, cut in ¼ inch rings
Parsnips, peeled and cut into sticks
Asparagus tips
Turnips, peeled and cubed
Pea pods, ends trimmed and strings removed if necessary
Green beans, ends trimmed
Eggplant, cut in half. Cut away flesh, leaving ⅛ inch clinging to the skin. Cut the skin into fan shapes about 1½ inches long
Zucchini, cut in half lengthwise and then into thin slices across
Okra, stems removed and pods left whole
Broccoli, cut into flowerets
Cauliflower, cut into flowerets
Parsley, snipped into small bunches
Sweet potato, peeled and sliced into ½ inch rounds
Carrots, peeled and cut into diagonal slices
Cucumber, cut in quarters lengthwise and then into 1 inch wedges
Oil for frying

DIPPING SAUCE
½ cup chicken stock
4 tbsps soy sauce
4 tbsps sherry or sake
Pinch sugar
Small piece daikon radish, grated
Small piece ginger, grated

BATTER
1 egg yolk
1¼ cups iced water
1 cup all-purpose flour

Prepare the vegetables as directed. Mix all the ingredients for the sauce except the radish and ginger. Pour the sauce into 4 small bowls. Place a small mound of grated radish and one of grated ginger on each of 4 plates. Heat oil in a deep-fat fryer to 350°F (180°C). A wok may also be used. Beat the egg yolk lightly and beat in the water. Sift in the flour and stir with a table knife. The batter should look lumpy and under-mixed. Dip each vegetable in the batter and shake off the excess. Lower ingredients carefully into the hot oil and cook for about 2 minutes, turning once or twice with a metal spoon. Fry only 3 or 4 pieces at a time and fry only 1 kind of vegetable at a time. Do not coat too many vegetables in advance. Drain fried vegetables on paper towels on a rack for a few seconds before serving. Serve while still hot and crisp. Each person may mix a desired amount of the grated radish and ginger into the dipping sauce to eat with the tempura.

Taksuta-Age (Deep-Fried Chicken)

PREPARATION TIME: 15 minutes, plus marinating time

COOKING TIME: 2-3 minutes per batch

SERVES: 4 people

4 chicken breasts
3 tbsps soy sauce
1 tbsp mirin or sweet sherry
1 tbsp rice vinegar
2 tbps sugar
1 clove garlic, minced
2oz flour, with a pinch of salt and pepper
Oil for frying

Cut the chicken into 1 inch cubes and combine with all remaining ingredients except flour in a deep bowl and leave to marinate, covered, for about 1 hour in a cool place. Stir occasionally to coat the chicken evenly. Remove the chicken from the marinade with a draining spoon. Toss in the seasoned flour to coat. Heat the oil in a deep-fat fryer or wok to 350°F (180°C) and fry the chicken, a few pieces at a time. Cook until golden brown and crisp, about 2-3 minutes per batch. Drain on paper towels a few seconds before serving. Serve with extra soy sauce for dipping, if desired.

Facing page: Vegetable Tempura.

Fish Tempura

PREPARATION TIME: 30 minutes

COOKING TIME: 2 minutes per batch

SERVES: 4 people

12 uncooked jumbo shrimp
2 whitefish fillets, skinned and cut into
    2 x ¾ inch strips
Small whole fish such as smelt or
    whitebait
Squid, cleaned and cut into 1 x 3 inch
    strips and dredged with flour
Oil for frying

DIPPING SAUCE
⅓ cup soy sauce
Juice and zest of 1 lemon or lime
¼ cup dashi

BATTER
1 egg yolk
1 cup iced water
1 cup all-purpose flour, sifted

Shell the shrimp, leaving only the tail shell on the end of each. De-vein if necessary. Wash the whole fish and pat dry. Prepare other fish as directed. Mix the dipping sauce ingredients and pour into small

bowls. Heat oil in a deep-fat fryer to 350°F (180°C). A wok may also be used. To make the batter, beat the egg yolk lightly and gradually beat in the iced water. Sift in the flour and stir the batter with a table knife. Batter will be lumpy and look under-mixed. Dip each piece of fish in the batter and shake off the excess. Lower ingredients carefully into the hot oil and cook for about 2 minutes, turning once or twice with a metal spoon. Fry only 3 or 4 pieces of fish at a time, and only 1 kind of fish at a time. Do not coat too many pieces of fish in advance. Drain on a rack with

cubes. Heat the oil in a deep-fat fryer or wok to 350°F (180°C). Reduce heat slightly and add the tofu cubes to the hot oil. Deep-fry 1-2 minutes or until cubes float to the surface. Turn them over and fry a further 1 minute. Remove from the oil with a draining spoon and drain on a rack or paper towels. Cook tofu in several batches. Meanwhile, bring the stock to the boil in a saucepan. Add the beans and bonito flakes and simmer gently for 5 minutes until the beans are just tender. Transfer the beans to a serving dish with a draining spoon. Arrange them in a circle and keep warm. Rapidly boil the cooking liquid to reduce by half and pour over the beans. Pile the deep-fried tofu into the center of the beans to serve.

Chicken Croquettes

PREPARATION TIME: 20 minutes

COOKING TIME: 3-5 minutes per batch

SERVES: 4 people

8oz ground chicken
8oz cooked, mashed potatoes
½ small onion, finely chopped
1 clove garlic, minced
2 tbsps chopped parsley
Salt
Pepper
1 tbsp soy sauce
1 egg, beaten
1 cup breadcrumbs
Oil for frying

Combine the chicken, potatoes, onion, garlic, parsley, salt, pepper and soy sauce together in a mixing bowl. Add the egg and mix well. Form the mixture into small cylinder shapes about 2 x ½ inch. Roll in breadcrumbs and chill briefly. Heat oil to 350°F (180°C) in a deep-fat fryer or wok. Lower the croquettes carefully into the hot oil and fry for about 3-5 minutes, until golden brown and crisp. Cook in small batches. Drain on paper towels on a rack for a few seconds before serving. Serve with soy sauce for dipping if desired.

paper towels for a few seconds before serving. Serve with the sauce for dipping while still hot and crisp.

Deep-Fried Tofu with Green Beans

PREPARATION TIME: 20 minutes

COOKING TIME: 5 minutes for beans, 1-2 minutes per batch for tofu

SERVES: 4 people

Facing page: Fish Tempura. This page: Deep-Fried Tofu with Green Beans (top) and Chicken Croquettes (bottom).

1lb tofu
1 cup chicken stock
8oz green beans, trimmed
1 tbsp bonito flakes
Oil for frying

Drain and press tofu to remove excess moisture and cut into 1 inch

JAPANESE COOKING

VINEGARED FOOD AND SALADS

Spinach and Bean Sprouts with Wasabi

PREPARATION TIME: 15 minutes

COOKING TIME: 1 minutes

SERVES: 4 people

1lb fresh spinach, washed well and stalks
  removed
4oz bean sprouts

DRESSING
2 tbsps rice vinegar
2 tbsps sugar
1 tbsp soy sauce
½ tsp wasabi powder mixed to a paste
  with water

Cook the spinach 1 minute in a
covered saucepan with only the
water that clings to the leaves after
washing. Refresh under cold water,
press to remove excess moisture and
leave to drain. Combine leaves with
bean sprouts. Mix dressing ingredients
very well and pour over salad. Toss
lightly and serve in individual bowls.

Daikon and Carrot Salad

PREPARATION TIME: 25 minutes

SERVES: 4 people

4 small oranges
½ daikon radish, peeled and coarsely
  grated
1 large carrot, peeled and coarsely grated
1 small piece ginger, grated
Rice vinegar
2 tbsps sugar
Pinch salt

GARNISH
Radish flowers and leaves

Cut the oranges in half and squeeze
for juice. Measure the juice and add
an equal amount of vinegar. Add the
sugar and salt and mix well. Cook
over low heat to dissolve sugar and
evaporate vinegar fumes. Set the
dressing aside to cool. Cut a slice
from the rounded end of the orange
shells so that they stand level. Do
not cut completely through the base.
Scoop out the orange pulp and cut

**This page: Daikon and Carrot
Salad. Facing page: Bean Salad
with Sesame Dressing (top) and
Spinach and Bean Sprouts with
Wasabi (bottom).**

the edge in scallops or points if
desired. Mix radish, carrot and ginger
with the dressing. Leave to stand 30
minutes. Fill orange shells with the
salad and serve chilled.

Gold Salad

PREPARATION TIME: 20 minutes

COOKING TIME: 6-8 minutes

SERVES: 4 people

20 spears white asparagus, stalks trimmed
Salt

SAUCE
2 egg yolks
2 tbsps rice vinegar
2 tsps dry mustard
1 tbsp sugar
2 tsps cornstarch
4 tbsps dashi
Chopped parsley

Cut the asparagus into 2 inch diagonal pieces, leaving the tips whole. Bring 2 cups water to the boil. Add a pinch of salt and the asparagus. Cook 2-3 minutes. Asparagus should still be crisp. Rinse in cold water and drain. Combine all ingredients for the sauce in a double boiler or in a small bowl in a bain marie. Stirring constantly, cook over boiling water to thicken. Remove and stir or wisk until the sauce cools. It should be the consistency of mayonnaise. Divide asparagus into 4 bowls, spoon over the sauce and sprinkle on chopped parsley.

GARNISH
3 green onions, very finely chopped

Pre-heat a broiler, or cook over charcoal. Dry mushrooms well. Cut stalks off and sprinkle caps with salt. Cut the tofu into ½ inch slices. Brush lightly with oil on both sides. Broil with the mushrooms, about 3 minutes per side, turning once. Cut mushrooms and tofu into thin slices. Arrange on dishes and mix the sauce ingredients. Pour over the mushrooms and tofu. Garnish with the onion. Serve hot.

Okra with Garlic and Seven Spice Pepper

PREPARATION TIME:	15 minutes
COOKING TIME:	5 minutes
SERVES:	4 people

40 okra pods
1 tbsp soy sauce
2 cloves garlic, grated finely
Seven spice pepper

Wash the okra well. Keep stem end on and put okra into boiling, salted water. Cook 5 minutes. Refresh under cold water and drain well. Cut off the stem ends. If the pods are small, leave whole. If large cut on the diagonal into ½ inch lengths. Sprinkle over soy sauce, garlic and pepper. Toss and serve in small bowls.

Lima Beans in Tofu Dressing

PREPARATION TIME:	25 minutes
COOKING TIME:	5 minutes
SERVES:	4 people

2lbs fresh lima beans (weight when shelled)
Salt

DRESSING
1 8oz cake tofu
2 tbsps sugar
Pinch salt
2 tsps sesame oil
½ tsp soy sauce

Facing page: Okra with Garlic and Seven Spice Pepper (top) and Lima Beans in Tofu Dressing (bottom). This page: Gold Salad (top) and Vinegared Mushroom Salad with Tofu (bottom).

Vinegared Mushroom Salad with Tofu

PREPARATION TIME:	30 minutes
COOKING TIME:	3 minutes
SERVES:	4 people

12 large shiitake mushrooms, soaked 30 minutes
1 8oz cake tofu, drained
Salt
Oil

SAUCE
3 tbsps lemon juice
3 tbsps rice vinegar
6 tbsps soy sauce
Dash mirin

3 tbsps hot water
Black sesame seeds

Cook the beans in lots of boiling, salted water for about 5 minutes. Reserve the water. Rinse beans in cold water and peel off their outer skins, using only the bright green inner beans. Lower the cake of tofu carefully into the boiling water left from the beans. Leave tofu in the water about 5 seconds and remove with a draining spoon. Drain well, wrap in cheesecloth and press gently to extract all moisture. Blend in a food processor or blender with remaining dressing ingredients except sesame seeds. Pour over beans and sprinkle on sesame seeds.

Vinegared Crab

PREPARATION TIME: 25 minutes

COOKING TIME: 3 minutes

SERVES: 4 people

1 small cucumber, grated
1 large cooked crab
1 small piece ginger, grated

SAUCE
2 tbsps rice vinegar
2 tbsps dashi
4 tbsps mirin
1 tbsps soy sauce

GARNISH
Chinese cabbage
Grated pickled ginger

Sprinkle cucumber with salt and leave to stand 30 minutes. Bring sauce ingredients to the boil and set aside to cool. Pour into small bowls. Rinse and drain the cucumber. Press to remove excess moisture. Crack legs and claws off the crab. Remove the meat from the claws and leave the thin legs whole. Separate the underbody from the shell and remove the stomach sac and gills and discard. Scrape all the brown meat from the shell and crack the body into 4 pieces. Use a skewer to pick out the meat. Combine all meat with the ginger and cucumber and toss carefully. Arrange Chinese cabbage on plates or trays and pile salad on,

This page: Vinegared Crab. Facing page: Sushi.

leaving some of the leaves showing on each plate. Garnish with whole crab legs and pickled ginger. Serve the sauce for dipping.

Bean Salad with Sesame Dressing

PREPARATION TIME: 15 minutes

COOKING TIME: 2 minutes

SERVES: 4 people

8oz green beans, trimmed and cut in 2 inch lengths
Salt

DRESSING
2 tbsps sesame paste
1 tbsp sugar
2 tsps soy sauce
2 tsps rice vinegar
Black sesame seeds

Bring water to the boil in a large pan with a pinch of salt. Add the beans and cook for 2 minutes after the water comes back to the boil. Drain and refresh under cold water. Leave to drain and dry. Mix all ingredients for the dressing except sesame seeds. Spoon over the beans and toss lightly. Sprinkle on seeds and serve in individual bowls.

JAPANESE COOKING

RICE, NOODLES AND PICKLES

Sushi

PREPARATION TIME: 40 minutes

COOKING TIME: 18 minutes

SERVES: 6-8 people

RICE
2½ cups short grain rice
Small piece konbu seaweed
3½ cups water
1 tbsp sake

ROLLED SUSHI
4 sheets nori
½ cucumber
2 pieces pickled red ginger
Wasabi horseradish

LAYERED SUSHI
2 sheets nori
½ cucumber
4oz smoked salmon, thinly sliced

SWEET VINEGAR
8 tbsps rice vinegar
3 tbsps sugar
Pinch salt

Rinse raw rice until water is almost clear. Leave in a colander 1 hour to drain. Meanwhile toast sheets of nori over a gas flame for 1 minute to freshen. Mix wasabi with enough water to make a paste. Slice the cucumber in half lengthwise. Reserve one half and quarter the other half. Mix the sweet vinegar ingredients and heat slowly in a small saucepan until sugar is dissolved. Leave to cool completely. Bring the water to the boil in a large pan with the piece of konbu. Remove the seaweed as soon as the water reaches a rolling boil. Add the sake and rice. Bring back to the boil and cook for 30 seconds on high heat. Lower the heat and cook for a further 12 minutes, covered.

Turn up the heat again and cook for 5 minutes to evaporate excess moisture. Take the pan off the heat and leave to stand, covered, for 10-15 minutes. Transfer the hot rice to a clean bowl and toss with the sweet vinegar. Cover the bowl with a damp towel until ready to use. Place 1 sheet of nori on a clean towel or piece of wax paper. If you have Japanese

bamboo mats these are ideal to use. Divide rice mixture in half and reserve half, covered. Divide half the mixture in fourths and spread some on the sheet of nori across the end closest to you. Spread some of the wasabi carefully over the rice. Cut a quarter of the cucumber to fit the sheet of nori and place on top of the rice. Cover the cucumber with another layer of rice and press it around firmly. Fold the end of the nori over the rice and tuck in the sides. Roll up using the towel, paper or mat to help you. Roll tightly, tucking in the sides as you roll. Repeat with the remaining rice, the remaining quarter of cucumber and use the same method with the pickled ginger, leaving out the wasabi. Leave each roll to stand, seam side down, for at least 2 minutes before slicing into 4-6 pieces with a dampened knife.

To make the layered sushi, line 2 6 or 8 inch oblong pans with plastic wrap. Divide the remaining rice mixture in half. Press half of that into one of the pans. Place the nori on top of the rice and cover with another layer of rice. Slice the cucumber lengthwise into thin slices. Place on top of the rice. Cover with another sheet of plastic wrap and place another pan of the same size on top. Press down and weight lightly. Leave to stand 5-10 minutes before removing from the pan and slicing the sushi into 2 inch pieces. Use the same method with the remaining rice and top with smoked salmon. Arrange the rolled and layered sushi on a large serving plate and give each person a bowl of soy sauce for dipping if desired.

Chrysanthemum Rice

PREPARATION TIME: 30 minutes

COOKING TIME: 30 minutes

MAKES: 15 balls

1 cup short grain rice
1¼ cups water
3 tbsps soy sauce
½ sheet nori
1 tbsp toasted sesame seeds
1 piece ginger, grated
6 eggs
3 tbsps dashi
1 tbsp sugar
1 tbsp sherry or sake
Oil for frying
Red caviar to garnish

Cook rice as for Chicken Donbun. Sprinkle soy sauce over warm rice, toss and cover with a damp cloth. Pre-heat oven to 250°F (130°C), place a sheet of nori on a baking tray and let dry for 3-4 minutes. When dry, crumble the nori. Add to the rice with the toasted sesame seeds and ginger, and toss lightly. With dampened hands, divide rice into 15 balls. Place 1 ball in the center of a piece of cheesecloth, gather up the ends and twist cloth to form a firm ball of rice. Remove rice ball from the cloth and repeat with all the remaining rice. Dampen fingers and flatten the rice balls slightly. Cover with a damp cloth and set aside. Combine eggs, dashi, sugar and

This page: Sekihan (Red Rice) (top) and Chicken Donbun (bottom). Facing page: Chrysanthemum Rice (top) and Onigiri (bottom).

sherry or sake in a bowl and beat well. Lightly oil a 6 inch omelet pan or frying pan and heat. Add about 4 tbsps of the egg mixture to the pan and cook over medium heat for 1½ minutes, until edges are dry. Turn omelet over and continue cooking until set, about 30 seconds-1 minute. Transfer to a plate and repeat with remaining egg mixture. Let cool completely and then cut into thin

strips, about 3-4 inch long. Lay the omelet strips over each rice ball to form "chrysanthemum petals." Make a slight indentation in the middle of each one and fill with a little red caviar.

Chicken Donbun

PREPARATION TIME: 15 minutes

COOKING TIME: 40 minutes

SERVES: 4 people

8oz cooked chicken
1 cup short grain rice
1½ cups water
1 cup chicken stock
2 tbsps sweet sherry or mirin
2 tbsps soy sauce
8oz fresh mushrooms, sliced
4oz peas
3 eggs
1 tsp salt

Cut the chicken into bite-sized pieces and set aside. Rinse the rice under cold water until the water runs almost clear. Leave in a colander to drain. Put the rice and water into a heavy-based saucepan and bring to the boil. Reduce the heat and simmer, covered, for 15 minutes until the rice is tender and the water is just absorbed. Stir and leave to stand, covered for 10-15 minutes before using. Put the stock, sherry, soy sauce, mushrooms and peas into a saucepan and bring to the boil. Reduce heat and simmer for 1-2 minutes until vegetables are tender. Add the rice and chicken and stir gently. Beat the egg and salt together and add to the ingredients in the saucepan. Cook over low heat, stirring occasionally until egg is just set. Serve immediately.

Sekihan (Red Rice)

PREPARATION TIME: 15 minutes plus soaking time

COOKING TIME: 55-57 minutes

SERVES: 4 people

¼ cup a dzuki beans (small red beans), soaked overnight

1½ cups short grain rice
2 tbsps black sesame seeds

Rinse beans and place in a saucepan with 2 cups water. Bring to the boil and then simmer, uncovered, for 10-12 minutes or until beans begin to soften. Drain and reserve the cooking liquid. Wash the rice until the water runs almost clear. Soak the rice in half the bean liquid for about 2 hours. Reserve remaining bean liquid. Drain the rice and mix with beans. Spread both out on a plate in an even layer. Place the plate in the top part of a steamer or on a rack above boiling water. Cover tightly and steam 15 minutes. Uncover and spoon over about ⅓ of the remaining bean liquid. Re-cover and steam a further 10 minutes. Repeat the procedure twice more during cooking. Rice and beans should steam about 45 minutes. Toss the red rice to fluff it up and sprinkle over sesame seeds to serve.

Garnished Noodles

PREPARATION TIME: 25 minutes

COOKING TIME: 20 minutes

SERVES: 4 people

SAUCE
3 tbsps white wine vinegar
3 tbsps soy sauce
2 tsps sugar
½ cup chicken stock or dashi
1lb soba noodles
4 cups water

GARNISHES
Cucumber, diced
4oz small, cooked and peeled shrimp
Celery leaves
2 sheets nori, toasted and crumbled or shredded

Combine vinegar, soy sauce, stock/dashi in a saucepan and bring to the boil. Remove from the heat and keep warm. Bring water to the boil and add the noodles. Stir once and bring back to the boil. Simmer gently until tender, about 5 minutes. Drain in a colander and rinse with hot water. Divide the noodles among 4 serving

dishes and arrange garnishes on top. Pour over the sauce and serve.

Five-Colored Noodles

PREPARATION TIME: 25 minutes

COOKING TIME: 18-20 minutes

SERVES: 4 people

8oz ubon or somen noodles
4 cups water
½ cup chicken stock
1 carrot cut into diagonal slices
1 small turnip, diced
4 dried shiitake mushrooms, soaked 30 minutes, drained and stalks removed, and sliced
4oz green beans, cut into 1½ inch strips
2 tsps cornstarch
3 tbsps soy sauce
4 tsps black sesame seeds

Cook noodles as for Garnished Noodles. Rinse under cold water and drain thoroughly. In a saucepan, bring the stock to the boil; add carrot, turnip, mushrooms and beans and cover the pan. Simmer 8-10 minutes until just tender. Blend cornstarch and soy sauce together and add to the stock. Continue cooking until slightly thickened. Divide the noodles among 4 serving bowls and pour over the vegetables. Sprinkle with black sesame seeds and serve.

Onigiri

PREPARATION TIME: 30 minutes

COOKING TIME: 25 minutes

SERVES: 6 people

1lb short grain rice
2½ cups water
4 tbsps black sesame seeds
Seven spice pepper
2 sheets nori

Facing page: Five-Colored Noodles (top) and Garnished Noodles (bottom).

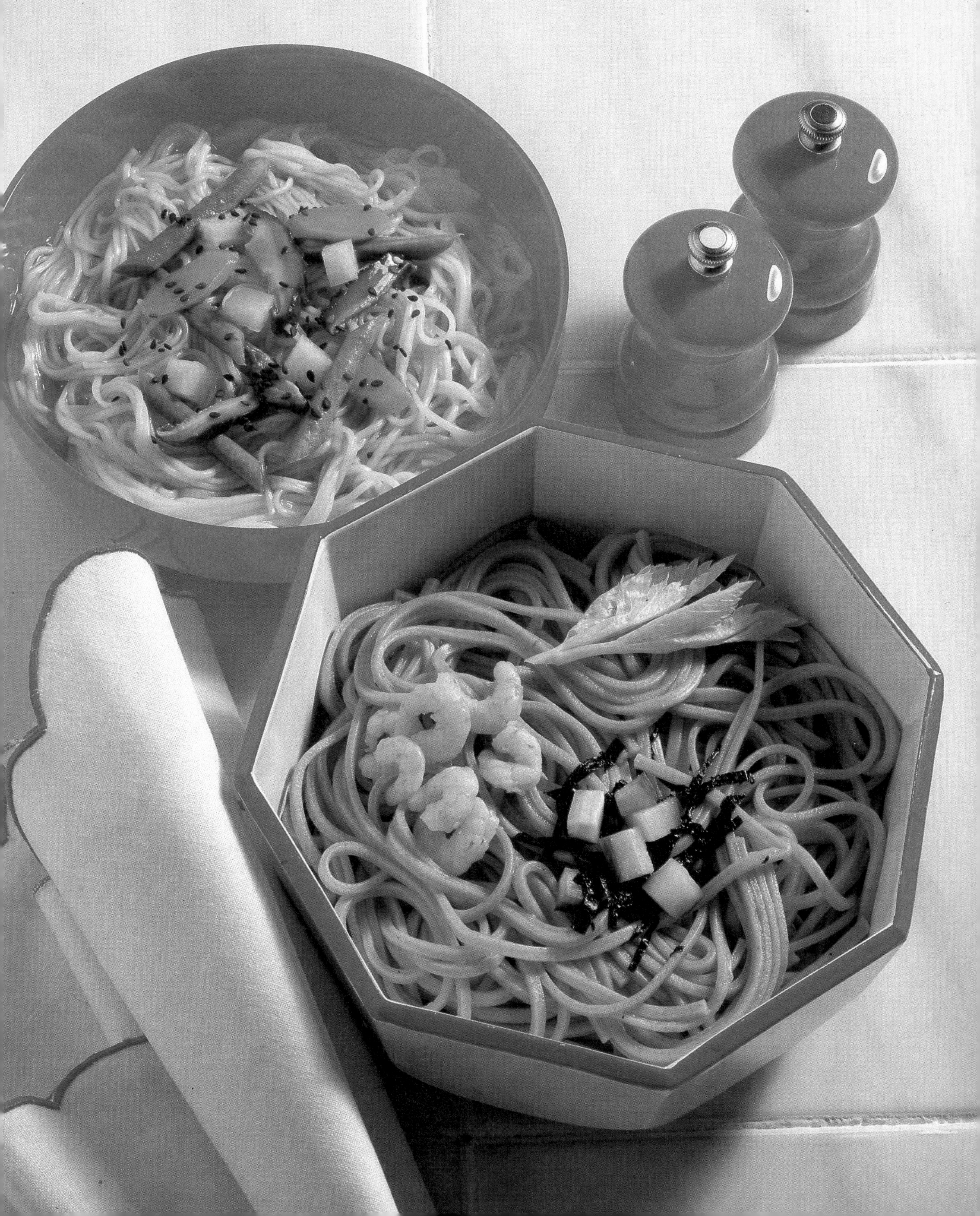

Cook rice as for Chicken Donbun. Dampen hands with salt water and shape hot rice into cakes, triangles and oblongs. Rice molds are available in various shapes and may be used instead of the hand-shaping method. Place the molds on a flat surface and fill with rice. Use the pusher to press the rice firmly into shape and then remove the mold. Toast the nori sheets over a gas flame and cut into strips. Wrap a strip around each rice oblong. Decorate one of the other shapes with black sesame seeds and the other with the seven spice pepper. Serve warm. In Japan, these are often eaten as snacks.

Cauliflower and Broccoli Pickles

PREPARATION TIME: 20 minutes

COOKING TIME: 3 minutes

SERVES: 4 people

1 small head cauliflower, cut in flowerets
4oz broccoli, cut in flowerets

DRESSING
1 tbsp wasabi horseradish
6 tbsps soy sauce
2 tbsps mirin
Black sesame seeds

Bring lots of salted water to the boil in a large saucepan and add the prepared vegetables. Mix the remaining ingredients and set aside. Cook vegetables about 3 minutes. Drain and refresh under cold water. Leave to dry. Toss with the dressing and refrigerate 3 hours before serving.

Cucumber Pickles

PREPARATION TIME: 30 minutes

SERVES: 4 people

2 tsps sesame seeds, mixed with 1 tbsp oil
1 cucumber
2-4 tbsps soy sauce
Bonito flakes

Spread the sesame seeds over the bottom of a heavy frying pan and cook over gentle heat until lightly browned. Peel the cucumbers and cut into 1 inch irregular wedges. Combine all ingredients except the bonito flakes and leave to marinate 20 minutes in a cool place. Sprinkle bonito flakes on top before serving.

Lemon Turnips

PREPARATION TIME: 20 minutes plus chilling time

SERVES: 4 people

4 medium turnips
Juice and rind of ½ lemon

This page: Cauliflower and Broccoli Pickles. Facing page: Lemon Turnips (top) and Cucumber Pickles (bottom).

Salt
1 small piece nori, shredded

Peel turnips and cut into large dice. Combine all the ingredients except nori. Put into a large bowl. Press a smaller bowl on top and weight. Refrigerate overnight. When ready to serve, refresh nori over a gas flame and shred finely. Sprinkle over the top of the pickle.

JAPANESE COOKING

DESSERTS

sugar until dissolved. Sprinkle on the agar-agar and whisk until dissolved. Dampen a 4 cup loaf pan and pour in the mixture. Leave in the refrigerator to set. Unmold onto a serving dish. Slice the kiwi fruit and arrange on top of the jelly.

Sweet Tempura

PREPARATION TIME: 20 minutes

COOKING TIME: 2-3 minutes per batch

SERVES: 4 people

Selection of the following prepared as directed:
Strawberries, hulled, washed and drained
Kiwi fruit, peeled and cut into ¼ inch slices
Apples, cored and cut into wedges, lightly sprinkled with lemon juice
Pears, peeled, cored and cut into wedges, lightly sprinkled with lemon juice
Pineapple, peeled, cored and cut in rings or pieces
Banana, peeled and sliced, lightly sprinkled with lemon juice
Plums, small ones left whole
Tangerine, peeled and segmented
Melon, peeled, seeded and cut into cubes or wedges

BATTER
1 egg
½ cup water
¾ cup all-purpose flour
¼ cup cornstarch

Clear honey

Orange and Kiwi Jelly

PREPARATION TIME: 20 minutes

SERVES: 4-6 people

1½ cups orange juice
½ cup water

½ cup sugar
2 tsps agar-agar
1 or 2 kiwi fruit, peeled

Put orange juice and water into a saucepan and heat until boiling. Remove from the heat and stir in the

This page: Sweet Tempura. Facing page: Orange and Kiwi Jelly.

Prepare fruit before preparing the batter. Pre-heat oil in a deep-fat fryer or wok to 350°F (180°C). Lightly beat egg and stir in the water. Sift in the flour and cornstarch and stir in with a table knife. Do not overmix; batter should be lumpy. Dip the fruit into the batter and lower carefully into the hot oil. Cook for 2-3 minutes until lightly golden and crisp. Cook in small batches and cook only one kind of fruit at a time. Drain a few seconds on paper towels. Arrange on serving plates and drizzle with honey. Serve immediately.

Nishiki-Tamago (Brocade Eggs)

PREPARATION TIME: 15 minutes

COOKING TIME: 20 minutes

OVEN TEMPERATURE: 325°F (150°C)

10 eggs
Scant 1 cup sugar
Pinch salt

Bring a large saucepan of water to the boil. Carefully lower in the eggs and bring back to the boil. Cook the eggs 10 minutes from the time the water begins to boil. Run cold water over the eggs until they are completely cooled. If prepared in advance, leave in shells in cold water. To prepare, peel eggs and push the whites and yolks through a metal strainer, keeping them separate. Egg whites can be finely chopped in a food processor. Mix the whites with a pinch of salt and about ⅓ cup of the sugar. Mix the egg yolks with remaining sugar. Place the whites in a square pan and press down lightly. Cover with the yolk mixture and press again. Bake for 10 minutes. Allow to cool completely and cut into 1-2 inch pieces.

Sweet Potato and Chestnut Pudding

PREPARATION TIME: 30 minutes

COOKING TIME: 30 minutes

SERVES: 6-8 people

10oz sweet potatoes, peeled and sliced
4oz can whole chestnuts in syrup
3 tbsps sugar
2 tbsps mirin or sherry
1 tbsp cornstarch
4 tbsps water

Soak sweet potatoes in cold water for 30 minutes. Place in fresh water in a large saucepan. Cover and bring to the boil. Cook about 20 minutes, or until very soft. Drain and dry over low heat, mashing with a fork or potato masher until smooth.

Meanwhile drain the chestnuts and reserve the syrup. Mix syrup with sugar and bring slowly to the boil in a heavy-based pan. Cook until the sugar dissolves and mixture thickens slightly. Mix half the syrup with the sweet potatoes. Cook the potatoes again over moderate heat, beating constantly with a wooden spoon until the potatoes thicken. Chop half the chestnuts roughly and add to the potatoes. Mound the pudding into a serving dish and decorate with whole chestnuts. Mix the remaining syrup with the mirin and the cornstarch dissolved in the water. Bring syrup to

the boil. Stir and cook until thickened. Allow to cool completely and pour over the pudding to serve.

Almond Sesame Cookies

PREPARATION TIME: 15 minutes

COOKING TIME: 10-20 minutes

OVEN TEMPERATURE: 325°F (150°C)

MAKES: 20

2 tbsps sesame oil
½ cup water
1 cup raisins
1 cup sesame seeds
1 egg, beaten
Few drops almond extract
½ cup sugar
1 cup all-purpose flour and 1 tsp baking
  powder
1 cup whole-wheat flour
20 whole almonds

Pre-heat oven. Place the sesame oil, water, raisins, sesame seeds, egg and almond extract in a bowl and mix well. Sift in sugar, the flours and

Facing page: Nishiki-Tamago (Brocade Eggs) (top) and Almond Sesame Cookies (bottom). This page: Sweet Potato and Chestnut Pudding.

baking powder, if using and mix to a stiff dough. Divide the mixture into 20 portions and roll each into a ball. Arrange the balls on a greased baking sheet and press an almond into the top of each, flattening them slightly. Bake 10 minutes depending on the number of cookies. The cookies should be crisp and golden when done.

JAPANESE COOKING

Almond Sesame Cookies 63
Baked Stuffed Trout 30
Bean Salad with Sesame Dressing 52
Beef and Leek Skewers 22
Beef and Scallion Rolls 10
Beef Roasted with Vegetables 30
Beef Teriyaki 24
Broiled Green Peppers 26
Butaniku no Dango 13
Cauliflower and Broccoli Pickles 58
Chicken Croquettes 47
Chicken Donbun 56
Chicken Livers with Cucumber 10
Chicken One Pot 36
Chicken Yakitori 22
Chrysanthemum Rice 54
Clear Tofu Soup 18
Cod and Cabbage One Pot 40
Cucumber Pickles 58
Daikon and Carrot Salad 48
Deep-Fried Pork 42
Deep-Fried Tofu with Green Beans 47
Egg Roll 26
Eternity Patties 40
Fish Tempura 46
Five Colored Noodles 56
Flying Fish 26

Fresh Vegetables with Sauces 7
Garnished Noodles 56
Gold Salad 50
Hakata-Mushi (Steamed Minced Pork) 32
Lemon Marinated Herring 42
Lemon Turnips 58
Lemon-Ikura 7
Lima Beans in Tofu Dressing 51
Miso Soup with Shrimp and Fried Tofu 16
Nishiki-Tamago (Brocade Eggs) 62
Okra with Garlic and Seven Spice Pepper 51
Onigiri 56
Orange and Kiwi Jelly 60
Pink, White and Green Rolls 10
Pork Kebabs with Vegetables 24
Salmon or Tuna Sashimi 19
Scallop Sashimi 19
Sekihan (Red Rice) 56
Shrimp Egg Custard 28
Shrimp Noodle Soup 16
Shrimp in Nori Packages 8
Simmered Chicken with Okra 36
Simmered Coltsfoot and Carrots 36

Simmered Flounder 34
Simmered Pork and Vegetable Casserole 40
Simmered Shrimp with Vegetables 38
Simmered Vegetables 34
Snowy Fried Shrimp 44
Soup with Fish Dumplings 16
Spinach and Bean Sprouts with Wasabi 48
Squid Sashimi 20
Steamed Abalone 30
Steamed Chicken 30
Steamed Fish Rolls 32
Sukiyaki 38
Sumashi Jiru (Basic Clear Soup) 16
Summer Chilled Miso Soup 13
Sushi 53
Sweet Potato and Chestnut Pudding 62
Sweet Tempura 60
Taksuta-Age (Deep-Fried Chicken) 44
Tofu-Dengaku 10
Tuna Sashimi 19
Tuna Teriyaki 24
Vegetable Miso Soup 16
Vegetable Tempura 44
Vinegared Crab 52
Vinegared Mushroom Salad with Tofu 51